AF745864

शहर या धुआँ

whispers of the soul in two tongues

Tushar Teji

BookLeaf Publishing
India | USA | UK

Copyright © Tushar Teji
All Rights Reserved.

This book has been self-published with all reasonable efforts taken to make the material error-free by the author. No part of this book shall be used, reproduced in any manner whatsoever without written permission from the author, except in the case of brief quotations embodied in critical articles and reviews.
The Author of this book is solely responsible and liable for its content including but not limited to the views, representations, descriptions, statements, information, opinions, and references ["Content"]. The Content of this book shall not constitute or be construed or deemed to reflect the opinion or expression of the Publisher or Editor. Neither the Publisher nor Editor endorse or approve the Content of this book or guarantee the reliability, accuracy, or completeness of the Content published herein and do not make any representations or warranties of any kind, express or implied, including but not limited to the implied warranties of merchantability, fitness for a particular purpose.
The Publisher and Editor shall not be liable whatsoever...

Made with ❤ on the BookLeaf Publishing Platform
www.bookleafpub.in
www.bookleafpub.com

Dedication

To all those beautiful souls

who nudged me gently (and sometimes not so gently)

to share my poems with the world –

even when they were raw, flawed, or just plain terrible.

Here you go.

This one is for you.

Preface

Poetry, for me, began not as a pursuit but as a response—a quiet rebellion against noise, a murmur when words failed me in the crowd. Each verse in this collection has emerged from moments I could neither explain nor ignore. Some were born under silences heavier than grief; others were whispered in joy too fragile to speak aloud.

This book was not planned. It happened — like rain, like longing, like a sudden silence in a noisy room.
Written across two languages and many nights, "शहर या धुआँ" is a map of inner journeys — across self-doubt and stillness, across fading memories and fleeting hope.

Some poems here speak in Hindi, others in English, but all of them begin at the same place: within. These verses are fragments of conversations — with the world, with a beloved, and often, with the self.
They ask questions that don't always seek answers. They sit with pain, sometimes with peace. And like the title suggests — they hover between what is seen (the city) and what remains (the smoke).

In writing these, I've tried not to decorate emotion, but to hold it – raw, brief, and honest.
If you find a piece of your own heart in these lines, know that this book has already found its way home.

Thank you for reading,
for feeling,
for staying.

– *Tushar Teji*

Acknowledgements

This book wouldn't exist without a handful of people who saw in my words something I hadn't yet seen.

To **my family** – thank you for being the roots from which every thought, memory, and emotion in this book grows.

To **Shikha**, who was the first to notice something in what I was writing – and the first to gently (but firmly) tell me to keep going, and maybe... publish someday. This book began with your nudge.

To **Bhavnesh**, for constantly pushing me to do better, to write better, and to never settle. Your words always made me want to sharpen mine. I miss you!

To **Rohit**, **Vatsala, and Priyanka** – thank you for your thoughtful feedback, for reading patiently, and for always believing in me.

To **Naveen**, whose own poems and reflections on spirituality often made me pause, rethink, and write from a deeper place.

To **Denny**, for casually planting the seed that this book could actually exist.

And to **BookLeaf Publishing**, for helping this little dream take the shape of a book — and for handling it with heart.

And finally, to everyone who has ever quietly felt too much — these poems are for you.

1. अब भी कोई बोलता है

अभी तो शाम भी नहीं हुई
फिर ये धुआँ कैसा है चारों ओर?
हम बैठे हैं सुनसान सी जगह पर,
फिर कौन मचा रहा है इतना शोर?

दूर दूर तक जहाँ निगाहें पहुँच पाएं,
ऊपर नीचे, दाएँ बाएँ –
सन्नाटों का दीप जल रहा हो जैसे,
फिर ये आवाज़ें आ रही हैं कैसे?

सोच सोच कर हुआ पागल ये कवि,
सर को हाथ में पकड़े है तभी –
जाने ना वो, है कानों में जो गूंज रहे...
उसी के तो ख़याल हैं सभी।

2. The Rain That Wasn't Supposed To Come

It rained,
When I thought it would not.

From a white, whimsical sky
And a black, belying cloud,
It poured,
When I thought it would not.

If truth be told,
It tried to hold
Back—
But it rolled,
When I thought it would not.

Lightning lashed the layers
Of the noble atmosphere.
The sound of a sulking sky
Swooned as it swayed
On the year's hottest day—

In the month of May.

It rained,
And rained,
When I thought it would not.

3. कहाँ हो तुम?

कहाँ हो तुम?
बे-ख़बर
धुआँ धुआँ

जहाँ भी हो
हो बे-असर
धुआँ धुआँ

ख़्वाबों की रेत पे सवेरे से
अनगिनत पाँव चल के आए हैं

गुम हो क्यों
रात से
धुआँ धुआँ

तुम भी गूँ
बे-वजह ही
आओ न...

ख़्वाबों को

कर भी दो
धुआँ धुआँ

4. In the Wake of the Storm

The storm of the day has long passed,
Windows of hope creak open wide.
Clovers by the porch stand green,
As the wind sings, afloat and free.
Look out at the barks in the woods,
Brown as they could ever be.
And those who know will agree:
It is all heaven, if it could be.

5. अज्ञात का हम-नफ़स

कभी यूँ करूँ कि ख़ुद से निकल कर ख़ुद को देखूँ,
फिर थोड़ी दूर चलूँ और ख़ुद से बेहतर ख़ुद को देखूँ।
घर से गली, गली से शहर,
शहर से बाहर, शहर को देखूँ।
फिर थोड़ी दूर चलूँ, और आऊँ दूर इतना निकल,
कि उसको देखूँ या ख़ुद को देखूँ, फ़र्क़ का कोई तर्क न हो।
फिर चलता रहूँ दिशाहीन, कि निकल के बाहर ब्रह्मांड से,
ब्रह्मांड को कण की तुलना में देखूँ।
फिर चलूँ मैं दूर कहीं, अज्ञात सी किसी राह पर,
और हो चलूँ मैं ख़ुद भी यूँही,
अज्ञात का ही हम-नफ़स।
अज्ञात का ही हम-नफ़स।

6. A Flare from the Sky

When the rain makes no sound,
But you know it's around.
You look for it anyway—
Through the window or the gate.
No, you're still not satisfied,
But from you, why would rain hide?
You jump out of your bed,
Fighting the quilt with your legs.
The only fear of coldness gone,
You run like one runs a marathon.
Now you're out there to face
The shining solitary sky.
There's no rain to taste.
You stand still for a while,
And just then, from heaven's bed,
A drop pours over your head.
Wohoo—You jump and scream,
As if someone's just added
A color to your hopeless dream.

7. बोझल रिवायतें

कभी ऐसा हो कि
बालकनी में बेख़ब्री ही कोई फूल खिले,
हर रोज़ सुबह की मीठी धूप
उस नन्हे गुल से आ मिले।
रात की रेशम सर्द हवा
भी उसके रंगों की बात करें,
रफ्ता रफ्ता कुछ यूँ हो फिर
बारिश की बोछार में,
नर्म नर्म पंखुड़ियाँ उसकी
बन जाएँ पंख बहार में।
के आए जब वक़्त निभाने का
मुरझाने की रिवायत को,
वो टूट के ज़मीं पे ना गिरे,
वो फ़लक की उड़ान भरे।
वो फ़लक की उड़ान भरे।

8. Whispers of Pain

Do the blooms embody your tears on a sad day?
For when you cry, the sky waters the land of lovers.
And when you lie awake, your arms hiding your face,
Lips touching the sheets, legs folded at the waist,
Do you feel the same as wine does when poured into a chalice?
For when it parts ways with the corked ocean, it breathes.
It gasps for just a moment before descending into the valley,
Where it cries for life, setting the skin aflame with its malice.

I love you, little hornet, even if daisies are your home.
For your mayhem's my solace, your silence my storm.

Ah, do these dry leaves, swishing in the street, embody your pain?
For when it rains and the winds crawl in, they will be

gone forever—
Like everything else.

9. मैं कौन हूँ?

मैं कौन हूँ?
ख़ुद से मैं ये अक्सर पूछता हूँ।
क्या मैं साँझ का पिघलता बादल हूँ?
या भोर की किरणों से लिपटा हुआ साहिल?
क्या मैं खिड़की से पर्दों को सरकाती ठंडी हवा हूँ?
या फिर फूलों के रंगों को चमकाती कच्ची धूप?
क्या मैं शोर हूँ?
या मौन हूँ?
मैं कौन हूँ?
...ख़ुद से मैं ये अक्सर पूछता हूँ।

10. Dreams, Tethered

Wires hold the mammoth oceans together,
While the wind's vile temper whips the weather.
A part of me knocks the knack on knots,
A part of me swims and sleeps forever.

In a rugged corner of a ruined ridge,
A raven perches up on the heathers—
And momentarily, brings to life
A man of a hundred feathers.

Years passed with a sprawl of seasons,
Withered winters and winds in rage.
A part of me ripped the book,
A part of me turned the page.

11. तुम अब भी यहीं रहती हो

खिड़की से बाहर पारिजात पर
दुधिया लगे फूलों ने
मुस्कुराना छोड़ दिया है
उन्हें लगता है शायद –
अब तुम यहाँ नहीं रहती।

अब चाँद भी उठता है
बस अपनी शक्ल दिखाने को,
सूरज जलता नहीं जितना बुझ जाता है
हर शाम।
तारों की भी अपनी ही फ़र्ज़-अदायगी है –
आते हैं फ़लक में नज़र,
बेसुध बादलों के बीच से झाँकते,
दो ही पल में चले जाते हैं।
उन्हें लगता है शायद –
अब तुम यहाँ नहीं रहती।

रंज-ओ-ग़म की नमी
मेरे घर की दीवारों पर भी
अपना निशान छोड़ गई है।

सीलन लगी इन दीवारों को भी लगता है
कि अब तुम यहाँ नहीं रहती।

बात थोड़ी संगीन है,
पर मुझे पूरा यक़ीन है –
कहकशाँ चाहे कुछ भी कहती हो,
...तुम अब भी यहीं रहती हो।
...तुम अब भी यहीं रहती हो।

12. The Betrayal of Blue

Can you trust the blue oceans?
For they are the only remains.
The grass is wicked green now,
And there's no water in the rains.

The birds don't fly anymore –
Their wings have been cut apart.
Winds once wild with freewill
Now search for reasons to start.

Hills have ceased to echo voices,
Now just heaps of falling rocks.
Even deserts, stripped of oasis,
No longer lend travelers hope.

Man has long been killing nature –
Now the roles are set to swap.
Fool be thou, if ye trust the oceans:
Black's the hue – blue color's a trap.

13. बात अनकही

रह गई उस रात की मुलाक़ात अधूरी ही
कहनी थी जो तुमसे इक बात, ज़रूरी थी
अब न जाने कब वो मौसम-ए-सौग़ात हो
अब न जाने कब वैसी हसीं मुलाक़ात हो
लफ़्ज़ों में जज़्बात दिन भर बैठ पिरोये थे
कभी सहलाए, तो कभी चाशनी में डुबोए थे
मख़मली में रखे तोहफ़े की तरह
दिल में रखे, दिल में रह गए
दुनिया भर की बातें कर लीं
और यूँ ही वक़्त के झरने बह गए

तलब है कि बन जाए वक़्त मेरा शागिर्द कभी
तो कभी उसे कहूं, लौट चले उस रात की गली
जहाँ वो मुलाक़ात अधूरी पड़ी है
जहाँ कहनी वो बात ज़रूरी बड़ी है
रख के दिल में हसरत फिर से वही
कहने जो चलूं तुमसे बात अनकही
कोहरे की इस बेशुमार गहराई में
तुम्हारे चेहरे से छलकती रुबाई में

फिर से कहीं ये वक़्त जीत न जाए
फिर से कहीं ये रात बीत न जाए

14. Another Fairy

She grew up to be
"Kid of the Year"
For ye kiddie, everybody
Made the cheer.

The mother was merry
With her only fairy –
Names of ye dear:
Susie, Sweety, Strawberry.

O' ye mother, one day
With thumpin' pray,
Wished to gift her
A baby brother.

The day of fates
Baked different story –
In ye lap of mother
Was another fairy.

The mother wore mood
Both mellow and merry.
O' for other traits,
'Twas day of hates.

What wrongs, wonders poet,
Hast fellow fairy done
That made mob mum –
O' fairy, why fairy,
Such whiny welcome?

15. वक़्त का सागर

हवाओं की तेज़ उथल-पुथल के बीच,
वो चलती है बेधड़क किसी सागर की तरह।
दी होगी आवाज़ कई हज़ारों ने उसे,
वो कर देती अनसुना किसी पागल की तरह।
नज़रों ने देखा है उसे धीमे चलते हुए,
तो कभी बरसे है वो घने बादल की तरह।
उसके चलने की आहट डरा देती है कभी,
तो कभी चुपके से सुनता हूँ – आदत की तरह।
वो बेज़ुबान नहीं, फिर भी ख़ामोश है,
वो जानती नहीं कि दुनिया बेहोष है।
स्थापित दीवार के दो कोनों के बीच,
कभी तीन तो कभी दो पैरों के साथ,
वो चलती ही रहती है – रुकती नहीं,
वो चलती है किसी सागर की तरह।

16. A Hymn to the Silence

Mortal gaze of the sun, from behind the skies,
Floating over curly waves, whispering goodbyes,
And a hymn to the silence from birds in flight
Surround me, lying by the empty shore.

I wake from a sleep within a sleep,
To whispers of dazzling domain of daisies,
Humming a mellow hymn to the Creator—
I dreamt of being a part of Mother Nature.

Of splendid serenity and surreal breeze, I dream,
Of a dozen deeds, but none to be redeemed.
I lay there a while more, as my soul
Dances with the dusk by the empty shore.

17. अस्तित्व

मैं बस विचारों का इक ढेर हूँ
जिसे बारिश सहला देती है
और धूप जला देती है।
ये विचारों का ढेर
सहला ने से सोता नहीं
सुलगने से मिटता नहीं।
यह साकित है, सतत है,
इस पे जादुई कोई परत है।
यह सदा है, या नहीं भी,
यह अभी है, या कहीं भी।
इसे भूख है बारिश की,
इसे प्यास है धूप की।
ये सच है या झूठ है,
जान लेना ही मूलभूत है—
ये विचारों का ढेर ही
मेरे होने का सबूत है।

18. Heart's Enmity

Blue, baffled brain,
Thinkin' all that's lame.
I hit the head with a fist—
It stopped thinkin' again.

There's smoke risin' out
From this filthy mouth.
I poked the sleepin' heart—
"What's this 'bout?"

"Don't you remember?
That day in December?
You shot me with a love dart,"—
Howled the heavy heart.

19. मैंने देखा है

मैंने देखा है,
मैंने देखा है लोगों को प्यार करते हुए,
पतझड़ के मौसम को बहार करते हुए,
मोहब्बत में दीवानगी बेशुमार करते हुए –
मैंने देखा है...

मैंने देखा है फिर उन्हीं लोगों को,
हुस्न-ए-इश्क़ का तिरस्कार करते हुए,
दरिया-ए-मरासिम में दीवार करते हुए,
बेवजह ही हदों को पार करते हुए –
मैंने देखा है...
मैंने देखा है...

ऐ देख न पाने वालों, मुझे रश्क है तुमसे –
ख़ुदा ने बख़्शा है जो अँधियार तुम्हें,
मुझे रश्क है तुमसे।
तुमने देखा नहीं लोगों को –
बेसबब बेवफ़ाई से,
बहुत ही सफ़ाई से,
बे-रंग सी स्याही से,

बेधड़क झूठ की गवाही से,
कल्म-ए-तबाही से –
उल्फ़त का कारोबार करते हुए।
तुमने देखा नहीं...
मैंने देखा है।

20. Arrival of Hope

On a hopeless summer day, within a savanna sea,
Through endless dawn, I waited – for loneliness to flee.
I lay on the softest grass that ever graced the Earth,
Kissed by the buried sands that slept through ages beneath.
'Twas when feathers fluttered and whispered a rustling wave,
The hues of hope found haven in the most sumptuous veil
I woke from the burden of thoughts, set still and pale,
And lifted my gaze... upon the Nightingale.

21. सच

धुएं की आड़ में छिपा हुआ ये सच,
बंद किसी किताब में लिखा हुआ ये सच।
सच, जो बेशुमार है, बेहिसाब है –
बेवजह ही हिजाब में लिपटा हुआ ये सच।

इंसाफ़ की लालसा में सुलगता हुआ ये सच,
ईर्ष्या की आँच पे उबलता हुआ ये सच।
बेबस ही बाग़ में मुरझा रहा कहीं,
काँटों की जकड़ में तड़पता हुआ ये सच।

एक तेरा सच, एक मेरा सच –
और न जाने कितने हैं सच!
इतने हैं सच... पर सच्चाई कहीं नहीं।
मुझे सच जानने की ख़्वाहिश नहीं रही।

22. The Happiest Blizzard

On days when the sun shivers
And stays back home – she
Comes out and dances for hours
In a garden full of daffodils.

Snowflakes swirl around her,
And petals from the purple pots
Curl around her feet. And along
With birds' tweets, she sings.

O, she sings like spring does upon arriving;
In a sea full of silence, she sings
About her wings – and the moon.

There, from the window, with gleam in eyes,
I watched in awe – this work of a wizard.
It felt serene, pristine, celestine –
Like a painting... of the happiest blizzard.

23. शहर या धुआँ

तुझे पाने की ख़ातिर
मेरा पूरा शहर बिक गया।
मेरे हिस्से में आई भी तो बस –
एक छोटी सी खिड़की।

अब जलती हुई शाम में बैठकर
कभी इस खिड़की के बाहर देखता हूँ –
तो तेरा पूरा शहर दिखता है।

मेरा वो शहर
जहाँ हर मिज़ाज के फूल खिलते थे,
हवाएँ मुस्कुराया करती थीं,
लोग खुश होकर मिलते थे।
ओस की नन्हीं बूँदें
मद्धम आँच की दीवानी थीं।
तुम थीं –
तो मेरे शहर की भी इक कहानी थी।
तुम नहीं –
तो ये शहर बस एक धुआँ सा है।

तेरी यादों के दीये से जो धुआँ उठता है,
हवा में घुलते ही महकने लगता है।
ऐसी खुशबुओं के सिलसिले
जब माथा सहलाते हैं,
पलक झपकते ही मेरे
... कई शहर बस जाते हैं।

24. Frozen Feelings

There's this heat in the skies which
Melts the ice in your eyes – and arrives
The ocean, that could've been a hurricane,
Which would've stayed for a while,
Wiping off the smiles – and a pile of 'em.

But there's this heat in the skies which
Mimics lullabies and sweetens the size
Of the cries prisoned in the frozen eyes.
Oh, the cradles that carry these skies
Of the wondrous world that could ever be –
May thou stay aflame, just the same,
So the eyes that foster frozen feelings
Could do nothing... but rain.

25. चाहतें

चाहत है,
कि मेरी लिखी हुई किताब के कवर पर
तुम्हारे चाय वाले गिलास के निशान हों।
बीच के कुछ पन्नों में यक़ीनन उदासी हो,
भीगे कुछ लफ़्ज़ों की स्याही से उठती
ये गवाही हो –
कि तुम कभी आँखों में सागर लिए आई थी...

अपने गालों के शबाब से फिर तुमने
कुछ पन्नों को रात भर जगाया हो,
ज़ुल्फ़ों के बादल भी हो जाएँ ख़फ़ा –
इस क़दर कविताओं को तकिया बनाया हो।

उन पन्नों को तुम्हारे होठों के गुलाब अब भी याद हों,
देखे हों तुमने जो – वो सारे ख़्वाब अब भी याद हों।

और चाहत है,
कि किताब के आख़िरी पन्ने पर
तुमने कहीं मेरा नाम भी लिखा हो...

बस इन्हीं चाहतों के सिलसिले में
ये किताब लिख रहा हूँ।

26. The Dance of Wind and Leaf

"Wait!" a maple leaf sang out
To the gust of wind,
As a musk deer closed in
Beneath her wet, red abode.
"Now?" the wind proposed.
The leaf smiled wide,
And with a sudden, gentle force,
They met –
A thousand pearls of morning
Showered like chandeliers,
Kissing the deer's head
And the dancing dandelions.

www.ingramcontent.com/pod-product-compliance
Lightning Source LLC
La Vergne TN
LVHW050823051026
849532LV00008B/3089
* 9 7 8 9 3 7 1 5 6 4 1 0 6 *